SIMPLE COOKERY

One Pot

igloo

Published in 2011
by Igloo Books Ltd
Cottage Farm
Sywell
NN6 0BJ
www.igloo-books.com

2 4 6 8 10 9 7 5 3 1

ISBN: 9780 85734 9 842

Project Managed by R&R Publications Marketing Pty Ltd

Food Photography: R&R Photostudio (www.rrphotostudio.com.au)
Recipe Development: R&R Test Kitchen

Printed in and manufactured in China

Contents

Lamb Shanks with Root Vegetables

Prep and cook time: 1 hour 30 minutes   Serves: 4

- 2 tbsp olive oil
- 2 parsnips, peeled and cut into large chunks
- 1 medium sweet potato, peeled and cut into large chunks
- 1 turnip, peeled and cut into large chunks
- 1 bunch spring onions (scallions), trimmed
- 2 cloves of garlic, crushed
- 4 lamb shanks
- ¾ cup beef stock
- ¼ cup water
- ½ cup red wine
- 1 tbsp tomato paste
- 2 sprigs rosemary, chopped
- 1 bouquet garnit

Heat 1 tablespoon of the oil in a large heavy-based saucepan, add the root vegetables and cook quickly until brown. Set aside on a plate. Add the extra oil to the pan and brown the garlic and lamb for a few minutes.

To the pan, add the stock, water, red wine, tomato paste, rosemary, bouquet garni, pepper, and salt. Bring to the boil, reduce the heat, and leave to simmer, with the lid on, for 20 minutes.

Return the vegetables to the pan, and continue to cook for another 30 minutes, until everything is cooked.

Before serving, remove the bouquet garni and check the seasoning.

Lamb and Sweet Potato Stew

Prep and cook time: 1 hour 50 minutes   Serves: 6

- 1 tbsp olive oil
- 12 lamb chops
- 1 litre / 33 fl oz. / 4 cups lamb stock
- 2 onions, thinly sliced
- 700g / 1½lb sweet potatoes, cut into 1cm (½in) thick slices
- 1¼ cups carrots, chopped
- 5 stalks celery, chopped
- 6–7 fresh sage leaves or 1 tsp dried sage
- 4–5 fresh thyme sprigs or 1 tsp dried thyme
- salt and black pepper
- 90g / 3 oz pearl barley

Preheat the oven to 190°C (380F). Heat the oil in a large, heavy-based pan and fry the chops for 1–2 minutes each side to brown (you may have to do this in batches). Remove the chops, discard the oil and add about half a cup of stock to the pan. Bring to the boil, stirring and scraping the bottom of the pan, then add to the rest of the stock.

Place half of the onions in a large ovenproof dish. Top with ⅓ of the sweet potatoes, then add half the carrots and celery and all the sage, thyme, and chops. Season, then sprinkle with the barley. Repeat the layering and top with the remaining sweet potatoes. Pour over the stock and cover.

Cook for 1½ hours, or until the lamb is tender, checking occasionally and adding more stock or water if the stew becomes too dry. Remove the lid and increase the oven heat to 230°C (450F). Cook for 8–10 minutes, until the sweet potatoes have browned.

Lamb and Prune Tagine

Prep and cook time: 2 hours 20 minutes   Serves: 4

- 400g / 14oz lamb, cubed
- 1 medium onion, finely chopped
- ½ tsp ground ginger
- 1½ cups chicken stock
- 1 cinnamon stick
- salt and pepper to taste
- 1 cup pitted prunes
- 1 tbsp honey
- 2 tsps grated orange rind

Cut a circle of baking paper to be 4cm (1½in) larger in diameter than the base of the saucepan being used. Line the saucepan with the cut circle, pressing it well into the sides.

Heat the saucepan on high heat, add the lamb cubes and onion and spread in a single layer. When the underside has changed colour, toss over to sear and seal the sides. Add the ginger, stir to coat the meat, pour in half a cup of stock then immediately pull out the baking paper and set aside. Add the remaining stock, cinnamon stick, salt, and pepper. Bring to the boil, immediately reduce the heat to a simmer. Place the reserved baking paper circle to rest on top of the meat to contain the steam, and simmer for 50 minutes.

Remove the baking paper and discard. Stir in the prunes, honey, and orange rind. Simmer, covered, for 40 minutes or until the lamb is tender. Remove the lid to reduce the liquid content for the last 10 minutes of cooking. Serve with steamed couscous.

Slow-Simmered Lamb Shanks with Couscous

Prep and cook time: 2 hours

Serves 4

- 4 Frenched lamb shanks (ask your butcher to do this)
- 400g / 14 oz / 2 cups chopped tomatoes
- 1 cup red wine
- 1 bay leaf
- 6 sprigs fresh thyme
- 1 cinnamon stick
- ½ a pumpkin, cut into large pieces
- 2 courgettes (zucchini), cut into large pieces
- 8 dried apricots
- 8 dried prunes
- 1 cup couscous
- 2 tbsps flaked almonds, toasted

Preheat the oven to 160°C (325F). Heat a large pan over a high heat and sear the lamb shanks in batches until browned all over. Transfer to an ovenproof casserole dish.

Add the tomatoes, wine, bay leaf, thyme, and cinnamon stick. Cover and cook for 1 hour. Add the pumpkin, zucchini, apricots, and prunes and cook uncovered for 30 minutes, or until the vegetables are soft and the lamb starts to come away from the bone.

Put the couscous in a large bowl, cover with 2 cups of boiling water and allow it to stand for 10 minutes or until all the liquid is absorbed.

Serve the lambs shanks on top of the couscous and garnished with the flaked almonds.

Slow-Cooked Lamb and Macadamias

Prep and cook time: 2 hours 30 minutes   Serves 4

700g / 1½lb boneless leg of lamb, trimmed of visible fat, cut into cubes

⅓ cup raisins

½ cup evaporated milk

Spicy Yogurt Marinade:

1 white onion, diced

⅓ cup ground, unsalted macadamias

2cm (1in) piece fresh ginger, chopped

½ cup plain yoghurt

2 tsps lime juice

3 tsps ground coriander (cilantro)

2 tsps ground cardamom

½ tsp freshly ground black pepper

To make the marinade, place the onion, macadamias, ginger, yogurt, and lime juice in a blender. Process to combine. Stir in coriander, cardamom and pepper.

Place the lamb in a non-metalic dish. Pour over the marinade and toss to coat. Cover and marinate in the refrigerator overnight.

Transfer the meat mixture to a heavy-based saucepan. Stir in the raisins and evaporated milk. Place the pan over a medium heat and bring to a simmer. Reduce the heat to low. Cover and cook, stirring occasionally, for 1½ hours.

Remove cover. Cook, stirring occasionally, for 30–40 minutes, or until the meat is tender and the sauce is thick. Add a little water during cooking, if necessary.

Serve with boiled rice and steamed vegetables of your choice.

Lamb Casserole with Couscous and Gremolata

Prep and cook time: 1 hour 30 minutes

Serves: 4

sea salt and freshly ground black pepper

2 tbsp flour

4 cups diced lamb, trimmed of excess fat

30ml / 1 fl. oz extra virgin olive oil

1 yellow and 1 green pepper, deseeded and chopped

400g / 14 oz / 2 cups chopped tomatoes

Gremolata:

1 clove of garlic, very finely chopped

3 tbsp fresh parsley, finely chopped

1 lemon, gated rind

Couscous:

2 cups couscous

1 tbsp extra virgin olive oil

Preheat the oven to 180°C (350F). Season the flour and spread it on a large plate, then toss the meat in the seasoned flour until coated. Heat the oil in a large pan and cook the meat over a medium heat for 2–3 minutes each side, until browned (you'll need to do this in 2 batches). Transfer the browned meat to an ovenproof dish, using a slotted spoon.

Add the peppers to the pan and cook for 2 minutes. Add the tomatoes and bring to the boil. Add these to the lamb and cook in the oven for 40 minutes or until the meat is tender. Meanwhile, mix all the gremolata ingredients together.

Prepare the couscous according to the packet instructions, then fluff it up with a fork. Add to the couscous and mix well. Sprinkle the gremolata over the lamb casserole and serve with the couscous.

Mediterranean Beef and Olive Casserole

Prep and cook time 8 hours   Serves: 6

1 lemon, juice and zest
1⅓ kg / 3lb lean braising steak, cut into 5cm chunks
2 tbsps olive oil
4 tbsp d black olives, pitted
4 tomatoes, quartered and deseeded
salt and black pepper
fresh parsley, chopped

Marinade:
2 medium onions, chopped
2 cloves of garlic, crushed
3 bay leaves
3 fresh thyme sprigs or 2 tsps dried thyme
1 tsp dried oregano
2 tbsps fresh parsley, chopped
1 small bulb fennel, chopped
2 carrots, sliced
8 black peppercorns
2 tbsps olive oil
750ml / 25 fl.oz white wine

Fill a large non-metallic bowl with cold water and add the lemon juice. Rinse the meat in the lemon water then drain well. Mix together all the marinade ingredients, then add the meat and coat. Cover and refrigerate for 4 hours or overnight.

Preheat the oven to 160°C (325F). Lift the meat out of the bowl, reserving the marinade, and drain well. Coat a large, flame and ovenproof dish with 1 tablespoon of the oil. Add half the meat and fry for 6–7 minutes, until browned, turning once. Set aside, then fry the remaining meat. Stir in the marinade and 3 tablespoons of the pitted olives and then mix together well.

Cover the dish with a double layer of foil, then a lid. Cook for 2 hours. Remove the lid and foil, press the meat down with the back of a wooden spoon and top with the tomatoes. Season lightly and drizzle over the remaining oil. Cover the dish with the foil and lid again and cook for 1 hour or until the beef is tender.

Skim off any surface fat. Season if necessary, then sprinkle over the lemon zest, parsley, and the remaining olives.

Steak and Kidney Puffs

Prep and cook time: 3 hours 15 minutes   Serves: 4

30ml / 1 fl. oz groundnut oil
1 onion, finely chopped
500g / 18oz braising steak, trimmed of excess fat and cubed
350g / 12oz pig's kidney, halved, cores removed, then cut into 1cm pieces
3 tbsps plain flour
1 tbsp tomato paste
2 tsps Worcestershire sauce
1½ cups beef stock
1 lemon, grated zest
2 tbsps fresh parsley, chopped
1 tsp dried mixed herbs
salt and black pepper
½ cup baby button mushrooms
1 pack ready-rolled puff pastry

Preheat the oven to 160°C (325F). Heat 2 tablespoons of the oil in a large ovenproof and flameproof dish, add the onion and cook for 5 minutes. Add ½ the steak and kidney and fry over a high heat, stirring, for 6 minutes or until browned. Keep warm. Fry the remaining meat, adding more oil if necessary.

Return all the meat to the dish, add the flour and stir for 2 minutes. Add the tomato paste, Worcestershire sauce, stock, lemon zest, parsley, herbs, salt, and pepper. Bring to boil, stirring, then cover.

Transfer to the oven. After 1½ hours, stir in the mushrooms and a little water, if needed. Cook for 35 minutes more. Meanwhile, unroll the pastry and cut it into circles. Put them on a baking sheet.

Take the dish out of the oven. Increase the oven temperature to 200°C (400F). Meanwhile, place the dish over a very low heat. Keep covered but stir occasionally. Bake the pastry for 20 minutes or until golden brown. Top each pastry circle with the steak and kidney. Garnish with the chopped parsley.

Steak Pie with Guinness

Prep and cook time: 3 hours 30 minutes Serves: 6

- 3 tbsp flour
- 1 tsp English mustard powder
- salt and black pepper
- 1 kg / 2¼lb stewing beef, cubed
- 60ml / 2 fl. oz vegetable oil
- 2 onions, sliced
- 2 cloves of garlic, chopped
- 2 cups Guinness
- 2 tbsp Worcestershire sauce
- 2 bay leaves
- 1 tbsp fresh thyme, chopped
- 1 tsp soft dark brown sugar
- 1 cup chestnut mushrooms, halved

Pastry Crust:

- 2 cups flour
- ½ tsp baking powder
- 2 tsps fresh thyme, chopped
- salt and freshly ground black pepper
- ½ cup cold butter,grated

Preheat the oven to 160°C (325F). Combine the flour, mustard and pepper, then coat the beef in the mixture. Heat 2 tablespoons of the oil in a heavy-based pan. Fry a third of the beef for 3–4 minutes, until browned. Transfer to an ovenproof dish and fry the rest of the beef in 2 more batches.

Add a tablespoon of oil to the pan, then fry the onions for 5 minutes. Add the garlic and cook for 2 minutes. Stir in the Guinness, Worcestershire sauce, bay leaves, thyme, and sugar and simmer for 2–3 minutes. Pour over the beef, then cover and cook in the oven for 2 hours. Remove the dish and increase the oven temperature to 190°C (380F). Fry the mushrooms in the rest of the oil. Stir into the beef, then transfer to a 15 x 20cm (6x8in) pie dish.

To make the pastry crust, sift together the flour, baking powder and half a teaspoon of the salt, then add the thyme and pepper to taste. Stir in the butter and bind with 10–12 tablespoons of water to form a soft dough. Roll it out, dampen the edges of the dish and cover it with the pastry. Trim, then make a small slit in the centre. Cook for 30–40 minutes, until golden. Serve with mash and peas.

Slowly Simmered Indonesian Beef Curry

Prep and cook time: 3 hours 35 minutes Serves: 4

- 2 stalks lemongrass
- 4 tbsp dried coconut
- 2 onions, chopped
- 2 cloves of garlic, crushed
- 5cm fresh root ginger, chopped
- 1 red chilli, deseeded and chopped, plus 1 red chilli, deseeded and sliced, to garnish
- 2 tbsp vegetable oil
- 700g / 1½lb beef steak, cut into 2cm cubes
- 1 tsp turmeric
- 475ml / 16 fl. oz /2 cups coconut milk
- 1 tsp sugar
- salt

Peel the outer layers from the lemongrass stalks, then finely chop the lower white bulbous parts, discarding the fibrous tops. Heat a large saucepan and dry-fry the coconut for 5 minutes or until golden, stirring frequently. Finely grind the coconut in a blender, or with a pestle and mortar.

Blend or grind to a paste the lemongrass, onions, garlic, ginger, and chili. Heat the oil in the pan and fry the paste for 5 minutes to release the flavors, stirring often. Add the beef, stir to coat and fry for 3–4 minutes, until sealed.

Add the ground coconut, turmeric, coconut milk, sugar, and salt to taste, and mix well. Bring to the boil, stirring, then reduce the heat. Simmer, uncovered, for 3 hours, stirring from time to time, until the sauce reduces to a rich gravy. Garnish with the sliced chilli and serve with rice.

Beef Braised in Rioja

Prep and cook time: 2 hours 30 minutes Serves: 4

- 60ml / 2 fl. oz olive oil
- 700g / 1½lb stewing beef, trimmed of fat and cut into 6cm (2in) chunks
- 6 shallots, finely chopped
- 2 cloves of garlic, crushed
- 2 stalks celery, thickly sliced
- 1½ cups mushrooms, thickly sliced
- ½ tsp ground allspice
- 375 ml / 13 fl.oz Rioja, or full-bodied red wine
- 55g/ 2 oz tomato purée
- 2 sprigs fresh thyme
- salt and freshly ground black pepper

Preheat the oven to 180°C (350F). Heat the oil in a flameproof, ovenproof dish and fry the meat over a high heat, stirring, for 5–10 minutes, until browned. Remove from the pan, then add the shallots, garlic, and celery. Cook, stirring, for 3–4 minutes, until lightly browned.

Add the mushrooms and cook for 1 minute or until softened. Stir in the allspice, wine, tomato purée, 1 sprig of thyme, and seasoning. Return the meat to the dish or pan and bring the mixture to a simmer.

Cover and cook in the oven, or over a low heat on the hob for 1½–2 hours, until the beef is tender. Season again if necessary, then serve garnished with the remaining thyme.

Rich Beef Stew with Shallots

Prep and cook time: 3 hours 30 minutes   Serves: 6

- 6 shallots, quartered
- 6 large cloves of garlic, quartered
- 3 large carrots, sliced
- 4 stalks celery, sliced
- 60ml / 2 fl. oz olive oil
- 1¼ kg / 2¾lb lean stewing beef, cut into 5cm (2in) cubes
- a few thyme sprigs, 1 bay leaf, 1 rosemary sprig and 1 strip of lemon zest, tied with string
- 375 ml / 13 fl.oz full-bodied red wine
- 1 cup beef stock
- 3 tbsp pearl barley
- 10 black peppercorns, crushed
- salt and black pepper

Preheat the oven to 240°C (460F). Place the shallots, garlic, carrots, and celery in a roasting tin, pour over 2 tablespoons of oil, and mix well. Cook for 15 minutes, turning frequently, or until the vegetables are browned.

Heat the remaining oil in a large, heavy-based saucepan. Add a third of the meat and fry for 5–8 minutes, until browned all over. Remove from the pan and set aside while you cook the remaining meat in 2 more batches. Return all the meat to the saucepan. Add the vegetables, herb bundle, wine, stock, barley, and peppercorns. Season and bring to the boil.

Reduce the heat and simmer, partly covered, for 2–2½ hours, until the meat is tender. Check from time to time and add a little more stock or water if the stew starts to dry out. Remove the herb bundle before serving.

Kashmir Pork Curry

Prep and cook time: 2 hours 25 minutes Serves: 6

- 750g / 1¾lb lean diced pork
- 1 tsp sugar
- 1 tsp ground turmeric
- 1 tbsp soy sauce
- 1 stem lemongrass
- 1 large onion
- 1 tbsp vegetable oil
- 4 cloves of garlic, chopped
- 1 tbsp ginger, chopped
- 3 tsps freshly chopped chillies
- 1 cup water
- 425g / 15oz chopped tomatoes
- 2 tsp fish sauce (optional)

Combine pork, sugar, and turmeric in a bowl. Add soy sauce and let it stand for 15 minutes.

Thinly slice approximately 7cm of the lemongrass stem and cut the onion into large pieces.

Heat the oil, lightly sauté lemongrass, onion, garlic, ginger, and chilli, add the pork and turn constantly to brown.

Add water and tomatoes, cover and simmer for 1½–2 hours or until the pork is tender.

Add the fish sauce and serve with rice.

Chicken Curry

Prep and cook time: 55 minutes

Serves: 4

- 2 cups coconut milk
- 1 cup chicken stock
- 2–3 tbsp green curry paste
- 3 kaffir lime leaves, finely shredded
- 1½ cups pumpkin, peeled and chopped
- 4 skinless chicken breasts, cut into small cubes
- 1 can bamboo shoots, drained
- 150g / 5 oz green (string) beans, chopped
- 1 cup broccoli, cut into florets
- 1 tbsp fish sauce
- 1 tbsp brown sugar, grated
- 2 tbsp Thai basil leaves, torn

Jasmine Rice:

- 280g / 10 oz jasmine rice
- 2 stalks lemongrass, halved

Put the coconut milk, stock, curry paste, and lime leaves in wok or large pot and bring to the boil. Cook over a high heat until the sauce starts to thicken slightly. Add the pumpkin and simmer for 10 minutes, or until it starts to soften.

Add the chicken and bamboo shoots, reduce the heat and simmer for 10 minutes, or until the chicken is tender. Add the beans, broccoli, fish sauce, and brown sugar and cook, uncovered, until the vegetables are soft.

Remove from the heat and stir through half the basil leaves.

To make the jasmine rice, put the rice, lemongrass, and 4 cups of water in a pot, bring to boil and cook over a high heat until steam holes appear in the top of the rice. Reduce the heat to low, cover and cook for 10 minutes, or until all the liquid is absorbed and the rice is tender. Transfer the rice to bowls, spoon over the curry and scatter with the remaining basil leaves.

Spanish Chicken with Chorizo

Prep and cook time: 1 hour 10 minutes Serves: 4

- 8 chicken joints, such as thighs and drumsticks
- 2 tbsp olive oil
- 1 onion, sliced
- 2 cloves of garlic, crushed
- 1 red and 1 yellow pepper, deseeded and sliced
- 2 tsp paprika
- 3 tbsp dry sherry, or dry vermouth
- 400g / 14 oz / chopped tomatoes
- 1 bay leaf
- 1 strip of orange zest, pared with a vegetable peeler
- 1 cup chorizo, sliced
- ⅓ cup pitted black olives
- salt and black pepper

Place the chicken in a large non-stick pan and fry without oil for 5–8 minutes, turning occasionally, until golden. Remove the chicken and set aside, then pour away any fat from the pan.

Add the oil to the pan and fry the onion, garlic, and peppers for 3–4 minutes, until softened. Return the chicken to the pan with the paprika, sherry or vermouth, tomatoes, bay leaf, and orange zest. Bring to the boil, then simmer, covered, over a low heat for 35–40 minutes, stirring occasionally, until the chicken is cooked through.

Add the chorizo and olives and simmer for a further 5 minutes to heat through, then season.

Cashew Butter Chicken

Prep and cook time: 1 hour 10 minutes Serves: 6

- 60g / 2 oz butter
- 2 cloves of garlic, crushed
- 2 onions, minced
- 1 tbsp curry paste
- 1 tbsp ground coriander (cilantro)
- ½ tsp ground nutmeg
- 700g / 1½lb boneless chicken thigh or breast fillets, cut into 2cm cubes
- 4 tbsp cashews, roasted and ground
- 1¼ cups heavy cream
- 2 tbsp coconut milk

Preheat oven to 180°C (350°F). To roast the cashews, spread them over a baking tray and bake for 5–10 minutes, or until lightly and evenly browned. Toss back and forth occasionally with a spoon to ensure even browning.

Melt the butter in a saucepan over a medium heat, add the garlic and onions and cook, stirring, for 3 minutes or until the onions are golden.

Stir in the curry paste, coriander and nutmeg and cook for 2 minutes or until fragrant. Add the chicken and cook, stirring, for 5 minutes or until the chicken is brown.

Add the cashews, cream, and coconut milk, bring to simmering point and cook, stirring occasionally, for 40 minutes or until the chicken is tender.

Chicken and Vegetable Casserole

Prep and cook time: 1 hour Serves: 6

- 340g (12oz) jar tomato and pesto sauce, or pesto sauce of choice
- ½ cup water
- 1 kg / 2¼lb chicken drumsticks
- 4 medium potatoes, peeled and quartered
- 30ml / 1 fl.oz olive oil
- 2 tbsp parsley, finely chopped
- 1½ cups frozen peas
- 1½ cups canned baby corn

Preheat the oven to 180°C (350F). Pour the tomato and pesto sauce into an ovenproof dish and stir in the water. Place the chicken in and arrange the potato quarters in between. Drizzle over the olive oil and sprinkle with the parsley. Cover with the lid, or foil.

Place the dish in the oven and cook for 30 minutes. Lift from oven and turn the chicken and potatoes. Add the peas and baby corn. Return to the oven and cook uncovered for 25 minutes more or until the chicken and potatoes are tender.

Tuna Macaroni Casserole

Prep and cook time: 1 hour Serves: 4

- 250g / 9oz macaroni
- 2 tbsp butter
- 2 tbsp flour
- 1 tsp salt
- 1 cup milk
- 200g / 7oz Cheddar cheese, grated
- 170g / 6oz canned tuna, drained
- 400g / 14oz frozen peas
- 100g / 3½ oz Cheddar cheese, extra
- 50g / 2 oz Parmesan cheese, grated

Preheat the oven to 175°C (340F).

In a large pot of salted water, cook the macaroni until al dente then drain well.

In a medium saucepan mix the butter, flour and salt. Stir until the butter is melted and ingredients are combined.

Add the milk and beat until the white sauce thickens. Add the Cheddar cheese to the mixture and beat until it has melted and the mixture is smooth.

Stir in the tuna and peas.

In a casserole dish combine the macaroni and tuna mixture. Sprinkle the extra Cheddar and Parmesan cheese on top and bake for 30 minutes until the top is golden.

Shellfish Stew

Prep and cook time: 1 hour Serves: 6

- 750g (1¾lb) frozen lobster tails
- 6 tbsps olive oil
- 500g / 18oz prawns (shrimp), shelled
- 500g / 18oz fresh cod, or monkfish, cut into chunks
- 250g / 9oz whole small squid, chopped into rings
- 1 small onion, chopped
- 1 red pepper, chopped
- 3 cloves of garlic, minced
- 3 medium tomatoes, peeled, seeded and chopped
- a pinch of saffron thread
- 2 tbsps parsley, chopped
- 1 bay leaf
- ½ tsp dried thyme
- 1 tsp chilli powder
- ¾ cup dry white wine
- ¼ cup lemon juice
- salt and freshly ground pepper
- 12 very small clams, thoroughly scrubbed
- 12 mussels, de-bearded

Cut the lobster tails into serving size pieces.

Heat oil in a large, flameproof, ovenproof dish and quickly sauté the lobster over a high heat for 3 minutes. Remove to a platter and set aside.

Sauté the prawns and fish over high heat for 1 minute and remove to platter.

Add the squid to the dish and sauté for 1 minute. Add the onion, peppers and garlic and sauté over medium heat until onion has wilted. Stir in the tomatoes, saffron, 1 tablespoon of parsley, bay leaf, thyme and crushed pepper and sauté for 2 minutes. Stir in the wine, lemon juice, salt and pepper and cook, uncovered, for 10 minutes. Add the reserved seafood, cover and simmer for 10 minutes.

In a covered pan, steam the clams and mussels with 2 cups of water over a high heat. As the clams open, remove them and add to the dish.

Hearty Bean Casserole

Prep and cook time: 1 hour 50 minutes Serves: 6

- 150g 5oz dried kidney beans
- 150g 50z dried black-eyed beans
- 1 tbsp vegetable oil
- 2 cloves of garlic, crushed
- 1 red onion, chopped
- 400g / 14 oz chopped tomatoes
- 1 tbsp ground cumin
- 1 tbsp English mustard
- 1 tbsp tomato paste
- 2 carrots, diced
- 3 courgettes (zucchini), diced
- 440g (1lb) canned butter beans, rinsed and drained
- 100g (4oz) broad beans
- 2 tbsps chopped fresh oregano

Place the kidney and black-eyed beans in a large bowl, cover with water and set aside to soak overnight. Drain. Bring a large saucepan of water to the boil, add the beans and boil for 10 minutes. Reduce the heat and simmer for 1 hour, or until the beans are tender. Drain and set aside.

Heat the oil in a large saucepan over a medium heat, add the garlic and onion and cook, stirring, for 3 minutes. Add the tomatoes, cumin, mustard and tomato paste and bring to the boil. Reduce heat and simmer for 5 minutes. 3 Add the cooked beans, carrots, zucchini, butter beans, broad beans and oregano to the pan and simmer for 30 minutes, or until
all vegetables are tender.

Vegetable Curry

Prep and cook time: 50 minutes

Serves: 6

- 60ml / 2 fl. oz groundnut oil
- 2 onions, finely chopped
- 6 cloves of garlic, finely chopped
- 2 pears, peeled, cored and finely chopped
- 3 tbsp tomato paste
- 2 tbsp mild curry powder
- 2 cups vegetable stock
- salt and black pepper
- 1 ½ cups baby carrots
- 1 ½ cups broccoli florets
- 1 ½ cups baby cauliflower, quartered
- 3 tbsp coriander (cilantro), chopped

Heat the oil in a large, heavy-based saucepan. Add the onions and garlic and fry for 6–8 minutes until golden. Add the pears and fry for a further 6–8 minutes, stirring and scraping the bottom of the pan occasionally until the pears soften and start to brown. Add a little water if the mixture becomes too dry.

Stir in the tomato paste and curry powder and fry for 1–2 minutes to release the flavors. Add the stock, season and bring to the boil. Reduce the heat and simmer, uncovered, for 15 minutes or until the liquid has slightly reduced.

Add the carrots, cover, then simmer for 5 minutes. Add the broccoli and cauliflower, cover, then simmer for a further 10–15 minutes, until the vegetables are tender. Sprinkle with the coriander just before serving.